CONTENTS

INTRODUCTION

It is often said that staff are an organisation's most important asset. This is especially true in a school, where children's welfare and the quality of teaching and learning depend on the people who work in it. Making sure that the most suitable person possible is appointed to every teaching and non-teaching post is therefore one of the most important tasks facing any school management. It is also among the most difficult.

If they are to identify the right person for every job, schools need selection processes that are rigorous, well-thought out and fair. They also need to be aware of the large and growing body of legislation that rightly bans unfair discrimination on the grounds of sex, race and disability. Although women make up the majority of the teaching profession, they are still under-represented at senior management level, as are teachers from ethnic minority backgrounds and those with disabilities.

In this handbook, we guide readers through the legal minefield of anti-discrimination legislation, the Human Rights Act and other relevant areas of the law. Drawing on our wide experience of helping both primary and secondary schools recruit and select staff, we offer practical advice on each stage of the recruitment and selection process. We also include model documents, ranging from job descriptions to candidate assessment forms, which you may wish to adapt for use in your own school.

Like other handbooks in the Education Personnel Management series, *Managing Recruitment and Selection* is aimed primarily at headteachers and members of the governing body's staffing committee. A chapter on the selection of headteachers and deputies highlights the role of governors in making these all-important appointments.

Maureen Cooper and Bev Curtis

The following icons are used throughout the book to identify certain types of information:

Case Study   Legal   Checklist   Model Procedure

CHAPTER I

THE EMPLOYMENT CYCLE

Staffing matters

Sound selection decisions are central to school effectiveness. Conversely, poor selection decisions are hugely damaging, as well as expensive. If the wrong person is appointed and leaves soon afterwards, it can cost hundreds of pounds to re-advertise the job. The senior management time required for what is sometimes a two-day selection process is much more costly. Add to that the damage that incompetent or unsuitable staff can do to children's education and - in the case of senior staff - to the running of the school, and the cost of a bad selection decision becomes incalculable.

Yet, whereas schools have always devoted considerable time and resources to choosing a new computer system or other major piece of equipment, when it comes to staff appointments they have traditionally relied on little more than an application form, a couple of references and a single interview. That has changed in recent years, and the trend now is to supplement interviews with methods that test whether applicants can actually do the job. For example, many schools now ask teachers to give demonstrations of their teaching, and set in-tray exercises and other practical tasks for applicants for management posts.

However, while selection techniques have become increasingly varied and sophisticated, there is still a tendency in many schools to view recruitment and selection in isolation from the wider task of managing staff. Our experience suggests that the most effective way of approaching selection is to treat it as part of an employment cycle in which each stage informs and influences the next.

This cycle begins when a vacancy occurs. The post is reviewed, a job description and person specification are drawn up and the vacancy is advertised. Appropriate selection techniques are then used to identify the most suitable candidate, and the new employee goes through a process of induction. Once this induction is over, the employee's performance comes under regular review, a process that is always easier to manage if the requirements of the job and the standards that the employee is expected to meet have been clearly analysed and spelled out at the start. Eventually, the employee will decide to leave. At this stage, an exit interview can determine why he or she is leaving. Information from this interview and from the performance management process can then help the school to define its future requirements and draw up a new job description, at which stage the whole cycle begins all over again.

The employment cycle

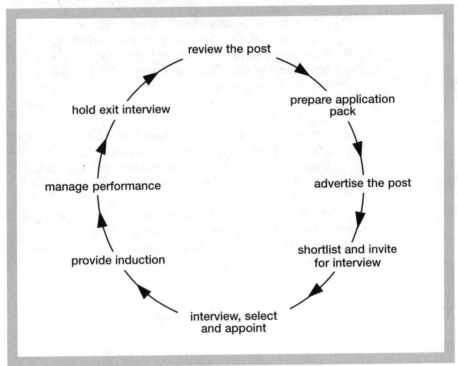

Reviewing what you do now

A useful starting point for designing effective recruitment and selection procedures is to look critically at what the school is doing now. The following checklist provides some of the questions governors and headteachers need to ask themselves when carrying out this 'health check'.

Checklist for evaluating recruitment and selection procedure

- Does the school carry out exit interviews to determine why vacancies occur?
- Are job descriptions reviewed whenever vacancies arise?
- Does the school always know what type of person it is looking for?
- Does it set out and use clear criteria at each stage of the selection process?
- Do all those involved in the selection process understand these criteria?
- Do job advertisements attract a sufficient number of responses from suitable candidates?
- Has the school considered using selection processes other than a single panel interview?
- Have all interviewers received training in interviewing and other selection techniques?
- Do the interview notes of all interviewers always show clearly why they have chosen one candidate in preference to the others?
- Are all of those involved in recruitment and selection confident that they do not discriminate unfairly between candidates on the grounds of sex, race, disability or other factors, including age?

If the answer to any of these questions is "no", there is probably a strong case for reviewing the school's recruitment and selection procedures.

The labour market and teacher supply

In a perfect world, all job advertisements would attract a strong field of candidates, and schools would be able to find the ideal candidate for every job. Of course, real life is not like that! The supply of people entering the teaching profession follows a cyclical pattern. When the economy is booming, competition for new graduates tends to grow and schools often lose out to other, better-paying employers. More experienced teachers, too, will sometimes be tempted out of the profession. In leaner times, the education service becomes a more attractive option; the supply of new teachers generally improves and experienced teachers tend to stay put. The supply of people for non-teaching jobs in schools also reflects the peaks and troughs of the wider labour market.

Recruitment is obviously easier when there is a good supply of teachers and others looking for work. However, during times of skills shortages, schools will sometimes have no choice but to appoint people who are not ideally suited to particular jobs.

Faced with an uninspiring field of candidates, headteachers and governors will sometimes decide to make a temporary appointment. This strategy carries risks because the law views non-renewal of a temporary contract as a dismissal and gives any employee with more than 12 months' service the right to claim damages for unfair dismissal. Unless an employer has a very good reason for not renewing a temporary contract, an employment tribunal may well decide that the dismissal was unfair.

To understand why the law takes this view, consider the example of a school that needs a science teacher who can teach physics to A-level but has been unable to find anyone with suitable qualifications and experience. A temporary appointment might be a way of covering the gap, but the school would need to explain very clearly to the individual appointed why the post is temporary. If the school fails to do so and later offers a permanent position to someone else, the temporary teacher will have effectively been dismissed. The reason for that dismissal can only be lack of capability, but if nobody had told the individual concerned that he or she did not have the right skills, experience and qualifications, the school will find it very difficult to justify the dismissal at that point.

Induction

Government regulations now require maintained schools to provide a one-year induction period for all newly-qualified teachers (NQTs). These new teachers are entitled to a 10 per cent reduction in their teaching load, and the time released in this way should be used to provide them with appropriate development activities. The induction period must also include half-termly teaching observations and follow-up discussions, half-termly progress reviews and termly assessment meetings. An induction tutor, who may be the school's headteacher or other senior manager, needs to make sure that records are kept of all monitoring, support and assessment activities, and their outcomes.

Failure to complete the statutory induction period satisfactorily means that the NQT is no longer legally eligible for employment as a teacher in a maintained school. Schools cannot impose this condition on other new staff but there is a strong case for giving guidance and support to all appointees. In addition, conditions of service for support staff may include a month's probationary period.

Even highly experienced teachers, including those taking on management roles, need an introduction to the ways of the school and how they are expected to carry out their responsibilities. Similarly, non-teaching staff need to learn how they are expected to do their jobs and deal with pupils, parents and colleagues. It will not be feasible to reduce every new employee's workload by 10 per cent, but if schools are to get the most out of all those they appoint, they do need to allocate some time specifically for induction.

Equal opportunities

Much of the legislation that we look at in Chapter 2 of this handbook is concerned with ensuring that people are not unfairly excluded from employment or promotion because of their sex, race or disability. Schools need to comply with both the letter and the spirit of this legislation, not only to avoid claims for unlawful discrimination, but also to make sure that they select employees from the widest possible pool of candidates. This is especially important when the labour market is tight. Every school therefore needs to make a positive commitment to promoting equal opportunities, preferably by drawing up a written policy. Ideally, this should cover not only sex, race and disability, the three areas where the law currently bans discrimination, but also age, religion, culture and sexual orientation.

However, a commitment to promoting equal opportunities should not be confused with the rigidity of outlook sometimes described as 'political correctness'. So long as people are selected by other people rather than machines, it will never be possible to eliminate all potentially unfair discriminatory judgements. After all, the purpose of any selection process is to discriminate - fairly - between candidates. What schools can do is to make sure that the processes they use do not lay them open to accusations of unfair bias. For example, a requirement to send in a curriculum vitae gives candidates the opportunity to include personal information that is not relevant to the job. There is then a risk that interviewers will use this irrelevant information to make their decision. It will certainly be difficult for them to show that they have not done so.

Asking all candidates for the same information, both on application forms and during job interviews, will reduce the risk of unfair or unlawful discrimination. So too will the use of selection criteria that are directly related to the job. When drawing up these criteria and writing the person specification for a job, selectors need to avoid vague requirements such as "must have a good sense of humour", which are only a short step away from the obviously discriminatory "must be one of us".

It is not unusual to hear interviewers discuss among themselves whether or not a candidate will "fit in with everybody". This does not present any real risk if all the candidates are able bodied or of the same race or gender, but if a minority of candidates are different in one of these ways, they may well draw the conclusion that they would not "fit in" because of their disability, race or gender.

However, while schools need to demonstrate the objectivity of their selection processes, they should not take this approach to absurd lengths. Reducing selection criteria to their bare essentials can result in an unmanageable number of applications, particularly for non-teaching posts, and will not help schools to identify the right person for the job. For example, a person specification for a school secretary needs to refer to somewhat nebulous but important qualities such as flexibility and discretion, as well as to word-processing speed and other measurable capabilities. So, although headteachers and governors need to demonstrate a clear commitment to equal opportunities, they should not abandon their common sense when making selection decisions.

Job-sharing

Staff shortages, coupled with the high proportion of women in the teaching profession and European legislation promoting equal treatment for part-time employees, mean that all schools now need to give serious consideration to requests for job-sharing if they are to fill their vacancies with the best people available. There is still resistance to job-sharing arrangements in some schools but those that have taken on two people to fill one full-time job - even at headteacher level - have often been very pleased with the results.

The arrangement gives job-sharers predictable working hours that allow them to meet family and other commitments, such as courses or other jobs. The school, on the other hand, benefits from having two teachers with their combined energy, skills and experience, rather than one. Job-sharers can also often provide cover for each other, in the case of absence through ill-health or attendance at courses.

This is not to say that schools should give preference to applications from job-sharers. They need to consider all applications entirely on their merits and appoint the most suitable person(s), but that is as likely to be two job-sharers as one full-timer. Obviously, with any job-share arrangement, both candidates must be able to meet all the requirements for the job. If only one of them is suitable, job-sharing will not be possible for that post and a full-time appointment will have to be made.

A job can be shared in a number of ways to suit the circumstances of both the two sharers and the school. For example, one may work mornings and the other afternoons, or each may work two and a half days per week. Each partner will normally work a consistent pattern, and it is helpful to have a handover period when both job-sharers are present in the school. Otherwise, their head of department or other line manager will need to make sure the partners have devised suitable handover procedures, such as meetings, notes and telephone contact.

If one job-share partner leaves, the post can be offered on a full-time basis to the remaining partner or the vacant part of the post can be advertised. The remaining partner may work full-time to cover until the vacancy is filled, or temporary cover may be used. If a replacement job-share partner cannot be found, the school should consider making the post part-time, based on the hours the remaining sharer can work. If the only option is to appoint a full-time person, then the contract of the part-time postholder will have to be terminated, but re-deployment should be considered carefully before the final step of dismissal is taken.

For a job-share arrangement to work, both partners have to take joint responsibility for the whole job, not just the duties they undertake individually. So, co-ordination and communication are critical, as the job-sharers in the following case study show.

Two into one does go!

When Dawn and Fiona saw an advertisement for a Year 2 class teacher at Stortley Primary School, they decided to apply on a job-share basis.

The headteacher and governors were initially reluctant to consider a job-share. They felt that parents would be resistant to the idea of their children having two teachers. However, at interview Dawn and Fiona were much stronger than any of the other candidates. The governors had taken personnel advice and, while there was no specific LEA policy on job-sharing, they had been advised that it might be regarded as indirect sex discrimination if the only reason for not appointing the job-share candidates was that they could both only work part-time.

The interview panel decided to appoint Dawn and Fiona, and worked out the job description very carefully to ensure that all responsibilities were covered. Fiona, who has two school-age children, now teaches all day on Mondays and Tuesdays and a half-day on Wednesdays. Dawn, a single mother who also looks after her elderly father, teaches the class for the rest of the week. They meet every Wednesday lunchtime to review the week's work so far and discuss what Dawn will do next.

Communication is the winning ingredient in this arrangement. Fiona and Dawn have developed systems for regular communication through written memos and, very recently, e-mail. "We do a lot of work behind the scenes to make this a success," says Fiona. "We keep very good records of any problems, summarise the day's events and keep lists and documents relating to what has happened."

Occasionally, in the evenings, they speak by phone to go over the day's events. Both women say they put in a few hours beyond what they are paid for, but say the extra time is a small price to pay for the flexibility the arrangement affords them.

The school's head comments: "Initially, I was very wary of employing job-sharers! However, I now think that the children have benefited and all the parents are very happy with their progress."

CHAPTER 2
THE LEGAL BACKGROUND

It is at the stage of appointing staff that schools are at greatest risk of falling foul of legislation banning unfair discrimination on the grounds of sex, race and disability. The Human Rights Act 1998 gives job applicants further grounds for challenging selection decisions, and makes it even more important that all of those involved in recruiting and appointing staff to schools avoid taking any step that may be seen as discriminatory or unfair. This does not mean that they need to turn themselves into legal experts. Advice on the law relating to staff recruitment and selection is available from the organisations listed in Appendix A of this book, as well as from local education authorities and from private sector personnel advisers. However, to avoid making costly and damaging mistakes, headteachers and governors do need to have some understanding of the legal principles we discuss in this chapter.

Education law

 The most important piece of legislation in relation to appointing staff in maintained schools is the School Standards and Framework Act 1998 which incorporates many of the principles laid down in earlier legislation. Schedule 16 of the Act, which applies to community, voluntary controlled schools and community special schools, and Schedule 17, which applies to foundation, voluntary aided and foundation special schools, give governing bodies full responsibility for appointing teaching and non-teaching staff whose

salaries come out of the school budget. However, the governing body may delegate appointments to:

- one or more governors, for example a staffing or personnel committee;
- the headteacher;
- one or more governors and the headteacher acting together.

The 1998 Act lays down the following procedure for appointing teaching and non-teaching staff to community or voluntary controlled schools.

1. When a vacancy occurs, the local education authority may give advice but is not required to do so. If it does give advice, the governors are under a duty to consider it.

2. The governing body draws up a specification for the post in consultation with the headteacher and sends a copy to the LEA.

3. The LEA may nominate candidates for the governors' consideration, for example a teacher made redundant from one of the authority's other schools. The governors are not required to appoint an LEA-nominated candidate. They must, however, consider any such nominated candidate.

4. Unless the governors decide to appoint an internal candidate or one nominated by the LEA, they must advertise the post.

5. Governors interview candidates and recommend an appointment to the LEA which, despite having no day-to-day responsibility for managing staff in community and voluntary controlled schools, is legally their employer.

6. If governors are unable to make an appointment, the post must be re-advertised and further interviews conducted.

Where the governing body of a foundation or voluntary aided school has given the LEA advisory rights, the procedure for appointing teaching staff is the same as it is in community and voluntary controlled schools. Where the LEA has not been given advisory rights, it must still be informed of any vacancies and of the names of shortlisted candidates.

The legal requirements for appointing headteachers and deputies are considered in Chapter 5.

Equal opportunities legislation

 Job applicants of both sexes and of all racial groups have a right to equal treatment at all stages of the recruitment and selection process. The Sex Discrimination Act 1975 and the Race Relations Act 1976 make it unlawful to discriminate against job applicants on the grounds of sex, marital status and race. The only exception to this rule is known as a 'genuine occupational qualification', which allows employers to restrict recruitment to members of specific groups. For example, if an adolescent boy with special educational needs had to be helped with toileting, a school would be justified in advertising for a male carer.

There may also be a case for appointing people from particular ethnic groups for some jobs funded by ethnic minority achievement grants (EMAGs). However, there has to be a genuine occupational qualification. In a recent case where a teacher made an unsuccessful claim for unfair dismissal and race discrimination, an employment tribunal rejected the suggestion that he should have been selected for the job in question just because his race would have made him a good role model. The tribunal ruled that, where there was no genuine occupational qualification, it would have been an act of race discrimination for the school to have taken the applicant's race into account.

In addition to the now familiar race and sex equality legislation, the Disability Discrimination Act 1995 makes it unlawful for employers to discriminate unjustifiably against job applicants on the grounds of disability. However, in schools, all offers of employment are subject to a satisfactory medical assessment of the successful candidate. If this assessment shows that the candidate has a disability that will impair his or her ability to do the job in question, discrimination may be justified if it is not possible to make a "reasonable adjustment". The Act requires employers to make 'reasonable adjustments' to employment arrangements or premises if these put people with disabilities at a substantial disadvantage to others.

Types of discrimination

 Unlawful discrimination can be either direct or indirect. Direct discrimination occurs when a person is treated less favourably than others on the grounds of sex, marital status, race or disability. Indirect discrimination occurs where people are treated equally but the treatment has an unequal effect on members of a particular group. For example, an employment tribunal has held that the rejection of a job-share application which a school could not justify on objective grounds amounted to indirect sex discrimination, since fewer women than men were able to comply with a requirement to work full-time.

Discrimination can occur at any stage of the recruitment and selection process, even before a candidate has set foot in the school. For example, an application form which asks applicants for their 'Christian', rather than 'fore' names may be held to discriminate against non-Christian candidates and, by implication, those who belong to certain ethnic minority groups. Care must be taken that advertisements, job descriptions and person specifications are not worded in such a way that applications from members of one sex or from certain ethnic groups are discouraged from applying. A person specification that refers to the desired candidate as 'he', for example, could be interpreted as discriminating against women.

It is also important that selection and shortlisting criteria and interview questions do not reflect assumptions about applicants' potential based on their race, sex, marital status or physical disabilities.

Where a job applicant - or an existing employee, for that matter - proves that he or she has been the victim of unlawful discrimination on the grounds of sex, race or disability, there is no limit to the amount of compensation that an employment tribunal may award. Six figure awards have been made in a number of high profile cases in recent years.

Damages can be awarded simply for the distress that discriminatory questions cause applicants. Although awards in these circumstances are unlikely to come to more than a few hundred pounds, headteachers and governors need to appreciate that asking women candidates about their childcare arrangements or partner's job, for example, may result in a claim for damages.

Local education authorities will usually foot the bill when awards are made against community and voluntary controlled schools. However, if a school wilfully ignores the LEA's advice and unlawfully discriminates against a job applicant, the authority has the right to deduct any sums awarded as compensation from the school's budget. Foundation schools may be liable to pay damages out of their own budgets, even if they have accorded advisory rights to the LEA. So, failure to abide by equal opportunities legislation can have serious financial implications for all types of schools. The bad publicity that a successful discrimination claim is bound to generate is also likely to damage the school's ability to attract and retain good staff in the future.

While the law does not yet ban discrimination on the grounds of age, the European Convention on Human Rights, now incorporated into UK law by the Human Rights Act, prohibits public bodies from discriminating against individuals on a wide range of grounds. Employers who specify upper age limits in advertisements or discriminate on grounds of age in other ways may, therefore, face legal challenges.

Within a few years, there will be even more grounds on which employees can bring challenges. The Equal Treatment Directive 2000 requires the UK to introduce legislation to prohibit discrimination on the grounds of religion, belief, or sexual orientation by 2 December 2003, followed by similar legislation relating to disability and age by 2 December 2006.

Quite apart from any legal considerations, it is good employment practice to welcome applications from candidates of all ages. The Government has issued a code of practice: *Code of Practice on Age Diversity in Employment* which is intended to help employers to choose, retain and develop the best person for each job by eliminating age as an employment criterion. As the introduction to the code points out, Britain has an ageing population and basing job decisions on age can reduce an employer's choice of candidates by up to a quarter. The code of conduct can be accessed on the Department for Education and Employment's website: www.dfee.gov.uk.

The Human Rights Act 1998

The Human Rights Act 1998, which came into force in October 2000, gives effect to the European Convention on Human Rights and in time is expected to have far-reaching effects on UK employment law and practice.

The Act applies to 'public bodies', a category that includes the governing bodies of maintained schools. Public bodies are required to act in accordance with the Convention, which gives individuals a number of basic rights, including the right to privacy in their family life and the right to freedom of expression. These rights may be infringed by some of the questions routinely asked on application forms and during job interviews. Asking candidates whether they have children or dependants, for example, may be held to infringe their right to a private family life. Similarly, questions about membership of clubs and societies, including political parties or trade unions, may be seen as an attempt to restrict applicants' rights to freedom of assembly and association.

The precise ramifications of the Human Rights Act will become clearer as the courts interpret it over the coming years. Meanwhile, the wisest course for schools is to ask applicants only questions that are relevant to the job and avoid any that might be seen as over-intrusive.

The Data Protection Act 1998

This Act repeals the Data Protection Act 1984. It regulates the use, not only of computer data, but also of manual and paper records kept as part of a 'relevant filing system'. In practice, this includes card indexes, microfiche and manual personnel files of the kind commonly kept by schools. In relation to the subject of this book, 'data' includes opinions about a candidate's performance at interview or on their suitability for a job. Confidential references given by previous employers or others are exempt from the new data protection regime, though it remains to be seen whether this exemption survives legal challenges brought under the Human Rights Act.

The Data Protection Act gives employees the right to see copies of their personnel files and to correct any inaccurate information they contain. Unsuccessful job applicants have a similar right in relation to information about them gathered in the course of the selection process.

The Asylum and Immigration Act 1996

Under Section 8 of the Asylum and Immigration Act, it is a criminal offence to employ a person aged 16 or over who is subject to immigration controls and does not hold a valid work permit. This offence applies only to appointments made after 27 January 1997.

An employer can mount a successful defence by demonstrating that he or she did not know that the person appointed was subject to immigration controls. In order to establish a defence if it becomes necessary, schools should therefore keep a copy of **one** of the following:

- a national insurance number (a temporary NI number, made up of the letters TN, the employee's date of birth and the letter F or M would not be sufficient);
- a passport or other official document describing the holder as a citizen of the United Kingdom or other European Union member state;
- a birth certificate issued in the UK or the Republic of Ireland;
- a work permit or other approval to take employment issued by the DfEE.

Schools should contact their personnel advisers on matters relating to this legislation.

Child protection law

Schools are required to do all they can to avoid appointing people who represent a danger to children and young people. In the past, police checks had to be carried out on anyone offered a post giving substantial access to children. Under a system introduced in 2001, employers can ask successful job candidates to apply for a criminal record check. This is carried out by the Criminal Records Bureau and can be used by the employer to help establish whether the candidate has a background that might make him or her unsuitable for the job (or voluntary position) in question. All application forms for jobs that give substantial access to children should seek candidates' agreement to a criminal record check.

If this check reveals that the candidate has been cautioned or convicted of a criminal offence, the head should seek advice from the LEA or the school's legal adviser. However, it is up to the governors and the head - not the LEA or any other external agency - to decide whether or not to employ someone who has a criminal record but has not been barred from working with children.

When the information provided by the Criminal Records Bureau differs from that provided by the successful applicant, the discrepancy should be discussed with the applicant before a decision is reached on whether to make the appointment or ask the police for further information.

The Department for Education and Employment and the Department for Health both keep lists of people who have been barred from working with children or young people. Before appointing a teacher, other employee or volunteer who will come into regular contact with children, schools must check that the successful applicant's name does not appear on either list. From the academic year 2001/02, these checks will be carried out by the Criminal Records Bureau.

Further information on the implications of child protection legislation for staff appointments can be found in another handbook in the Education Personnel Management series, *Managing Allegations Against Staff*.

CHAPTER 3
STARTING THE
EMPLOYMENT CYCLE

As we have already mentioned, recruitment and selection should not be seen in isolation, but as stages in an employment cycle. This cycle begins with the creation of a new post or the departure of the previous post-holder.

Reviewing the post

Very often, when a member of staff resigns, his or her old job description is dusted down and recycled. However, most jobs change over time, and an out-of-date job description will not help the school to determine what it is looking for from a prospective employee. Nor will it give potential applicants the accurate information they need in order to decide whether or not to apply. So, an employee's departure should be treated as an opportunity to review the post and ask whether its requirements have changed.

When carrying out this review, school managers also need to consider how the job fits in to the school's overall staffing structure. For example, in a secondary school, the departure of one or more heads of department may be an opportunity to move to a new faculty structure.

Exit interviews or questionnaires can help in the job-review process. People resign from jobs for a variety of reasons, including retirement, ill-health or the relocation of a partner to another part of the country. Sometimes, however, they leave for reasons that may point to problems with the way the school is organised and managed. Conflict with colleagues or line managers, a sense of not being valued or a lack of opportunities to develop may all fall into this category. Staff who are about to leave a school are more likely to speak frankly about such problems than those who are staying on. They may also be willing to give an honest opinion about the organisation and perhaps suggest improvements. So, asking them why they are leaving or how their jobs might have been improved can provide managers with valuable insights.

Exit interviews can also help to establish if staff are leaving for reasons that might lead to a claim against the school, for example for constructive dismissal. In relation to the subject of this book, however, the main purpose of an exit interview is to discover if the job that the individual has been doing needs to be redesigned in any way - or if it should exist at all.

Model exit questionnaire

	Agree very strongly	Agree	Neither agree nor disagree	Disagree	Disagree very strongly
The area I worked in was pleasant and well resourced					
The quantity of teaching resources available was adequate for my needs					
The quality of teaching resources available was adequate for my needs					
My workload was appropriate for the job that I did					
The tasks that I did were appropriate for my job description					
Parents' evenings are well organised					
Staff/departmental/team meetings are worthwhile					
The school's behaviour policy works well					
The duty system works well					
Performance management arrangements work well					
Staff are appreciated and valued					
I would recommend the school to a friend					

Preparing the job description

A job description should set out the nature and scope of the job and the duties that the post-holder will be expected to perform. It should be flexible enough to be reviewed and updated if necessary, and should include a flexibility clause. Since it is difficult to foresee specific changes that may be required in future, this clause needs to be couched in terms that are fairly general, but not so general as to seem unreasonable. Examples of flexibility clauses are included in the following model job descriptions.

Model job description for a non-teaching post

Post title: School secretary/clerk to the governing body

Responsible to: The headteacher

Purpose of job: To provide effective secretarial, administrative and clerical support services

Main responsibilities:

1. To maintain, operate and review efficient administrative/clerical support systems.
2. To co-ordinate the allocation of work to clerical support staff to ensure that the needs and priorities of the school are met.
3. To provide secretarial and administrative support to the headteacher and senior staff in accordance with good secretarial practice.
4. To ensure the effective operation of the headteacher's personal office.
5. To assist in the maintenance of good relationships with staff, parents, governors, the LEA, contractors' representatives and external agencies.
6. To ensure the timely and effective service of the governing body to facilitate the efficient conduct of its business.
7. To perform as necessary other duties of a similar or related nature to those outlined above.

Model job description for a teaching post

Post title: Class teacher (primary school)

Purpose of post: To carry out the following duties in accordance with the school's policies and under the direction of the headteacher.

Teaching:
- To plan and prepare schemes of work and complete planning documentation.
- To teach, according to their educational needs, the pupils in your class.
- To set and mark work carried out by pupils in school and elsewhere.
- To promote the intellectual, physical and personal development of the pupils in your class.
- To participate in arrangements for preparing and assessing pupils for national tests and tasks.

Assessment, recording and reporting:
- To assess, record and report on pupils' development, progress and attainment.
- To communicate and consult with pupils' parents, and others with a legitimate interest in the pupils in your class.

Professional development:
- To keep your methods of teaching under review and participate in further training and professional development as a teacher.

Curriculum development:
- To advise and co-operate with the headteacher and other teachers on the preparation of teaching materials, schemes of work, methods of teaching and assessment and pastoral care methods.
- To take responsibility for National Curriculum subject(s)...........................(specify)

Discipline, health and safety:
- To maintain good order and discipline among pupils and safeguard their health and safety both on the school premises and when they are engaged in authorised school activities elsewhere.

Staff meetings:
- To participate in meetings relating to the curriculum of the school, its organisation and pastoral arrangements.

Cover:
- To supervise and, so far as is practicable, teach any pupils whose teacher is not available. (You will not be required to cover after the teacher has been absent for three or more consecutive working days, unless it proves impossible to get a supply teacher.)

Other duties:
- As a term of your employment, from time to time, you may be required to perform duties of a similar or related nature to those outlined in this job description.

The relationship between a job description and the successful candidate's contract of employment depends on when the job description is issued. When the job description is sent out with an application pack, it may become a focal point in any subsequent interview and so entitle the applicant to conclude that it sets out the duties and obligations of the job. So, once an appointment has been made, the job description becomes part of the contract of employment.

On the rare occasions when a job description is issued only after the successful applicant has taken up the job, it is important to ensure that the document is consistent with the nature of the duties already established. In order to avoid conflict or disagreement, the job description should be mutually agreed with the employee in these circumstances.

Preparing the person specification

After reviewing the post and preparing the job description, the school needs to decide on the kind of person it is looking for, and, in particular, how much relevant experience that person should have. The obvious answer is "as much as possible", but a candidate with 20 years' experience in a similar job may have already reached his or her full potential, and there could be a case for appointing someone with less experience but a great deal of potential.

When drawing up the person specification for a post, managers need to look at the composition of the team the successful applicant will be joining. Few people in schools work in isolation, and a team made up entirely of inexperienced people, however potentially able, is likely to be less successful than one made up of both 'new blood' and experienced 'safe pairs of hands'.

The person specification therefore should be based on a careful analysis of existing conditions in the school and of the post itself, rather than on the characteristics of the current or previous postholder. This analysis will help to ensure that the requirements are neither under- nor over-stated and that they do not unnecessarily and unfairly exclude certain categories of potential applicants.

Like the job description, the person specification is intended to help potential applicants to decide whether or not to apply for a job. It should therefore be included with all the other relevant information sent to applicants.

What should a person specification include?

A person specification should provide the following information on what is required:

- qualifications;
- type, length and range of experience;
- skills and abilities;
- personal qualities and interests relevant to the job.

These skills and attributes should be divided into those that are considered essential and those that are merely desirable in relation to the post.

Advertising the post

The improvements that many schools have made to their selection processes in recent years have not been fully reflected in the quality of their recruitment advertising. Most of the advertisements that appear in the education press are dull summaries of job descriptions embellished only by a few over-used and often meaningless descriptive terms. Senior jobs, for example, are commonly described as "challenging" and requiring "drive and vision". Since a non-challenging school management post suited to the laid back and indolent has yet to be invented, these terms tell potential applicants very little about the job and do even less to persuade them to apply! Nor is advertising of this kind much good at filtering out unsuitable candidates.

Effective advertisements are those that attract the attention both of the active job-seeker and the casual browser, who may not have thought about applying for a job and who needs convincing that a career move is a good idea. Persuasive recruitment advertising can also help to create a positive image or 'employer brand' for the school, which will encourage talented people to apply, if not for the particular job advertised on this occasion, then perhaps another one later on.

It is also worth noting that recruitment advertising offers schools a rare opportunity to tell the world about themselves, and at the same time correct any misconceptions that the public may have. A school perceived to be failing merely because it serves a deprived inner-city area, for example, may be able to use a job advertisement to publicise a favourable OFSTED inspection or other success.

None of this means that schools need to spend a fortune on expensive artwork and copywriting. There are simple things they can do themselves, such as using an eye-catching heading, speaking directly to applicants in plain English and accentuating the positive aspects of the job and the school.

Model job advertisement

The future's bright

for a headteacher at
Lyndhurst Primary School
Start: Sept 2001 Salary: Group 3 Negotiable Roll: 347
Located in Camberwell, London Borough of Southwark

If you're a head or deputy with the vision, practical skills and drive to make our school even better, we offer you
- A successful Southwark school that's aiming higher
- Fantastic children who achieve high standards
- Motivated, dynamic staff with a strong team spirit
- Supportive, committed governors and a first-rate PTA
- Superb on-site nursery with sensory garden
- Strong extra-curricular clubs programme, including art, choir, dance, football, French, recorders and steel pans
- Well-maintained Victorian buildings and play areas

Please call our admin office on 020-7703 3046 to receive an application pack, and to arrange an informal visit with the headteacher
Closing Date: March 2. Interviews: March 21

It is not only the content of job advertisements that matters. Schools can also benefit from applying fresh thinking to their choice of advertising media. Although funds for advertising are now delegated to schools, many continue to ask their LEAs to handle this part of the recruitment process. With their bulk purchasing power, LEAs can usually negotiate large discounts from newspapers. So, where the press seems to offer the most effective way of reaching potential candidates, it may be sensible to stick to existing arrangements if these offer best value.

Newspapers, however, are not the only media, especially for attracting newly-qualified teachers. These teachers tend to be the most computer-literate members of the profession and the most likely to look for jobs on the internet, where they can also find inspection reports, and other information that will help them to choose a school. A quick and inexpensive alternative to press advertising is to use an LEA or other well-publicised web site such as epm.co.uk to refer newly-qualified teachers to the school's own site. This in turn can provide NQTs with all the information they need to decide whether the school and the job are right for them.

Speed is another advantage of advertising on the web. Whereas the lead time for placing an advertisement in a weekly newspaper is usually just under a week, there is no such delay when it comes to on-line advertising. If a school's web site includes an application form, it can be completed and returned before a hard copy advertisement has even reached the newspapers.

Headhunting and the 'old boys' network'

Maintained schools are required by law to advertise posts that are not filled internally. They must also advertise nationally for a headteacher or deputy head, but there is nothing to stop them from headhunting staff as well. Although this practice is not yet as widespread as in the private sector, the use of recruitment consultants to identify candidates is becoming more common in the education service. In some cases, schools go through the motions of advertising, while actually relying on headhunters, especially to fill senior posts. Since no consultant can possibly reach as many potential candidates as an advertisement, this approach may potentially discriminate against certain groups. The same goes for recruiting on the basis of personal recommendation or through the so-called 'old boys' network' - as no less a figure than the Lord Chancellor discovered in 1997 when he appointed a friend as his special adviser without advertising the post.

Coker & another versus the Lord Chancellor and the Lord Chancellor's Department (1999 IRLR 396)

A woman solicitor complained that the arrangements for appointing the Lord Chancellor's adviser had discriminated against her on the grounds of her sex. She claimed that she was well qualified for the job and would have applied had she known about it. The Lord Chancellor faced a second claim from a law centre employee, who alleged both racial and sexual discrimination.

When these claims went before a tribunal, the Lord Chancellor admitted that he had imposed a requirement that the person appointed had to be known to him personally. The tribunal held that the proportion of women and members of ethnic minorities able to comply with this requirement was far smaller than the proportion of white men who could comply with it. Since the first complainant was a solicitor who might have had some chance of being considered for the post had it been advertised, her complaint of indirect sex discrimination was upheld. However, the second complainant's claims of sex and race discrimination were dismissed on the grounds that she would not have been a suitable candidate and had therefore not suffered any detriment.

While the exact circumstances of this case would probably never be replicated in a school, this finding against a senior minister of the Crown does illustrate the dangers inherent in headhunting.

Processing applications

The way in which a school handles responses to job advertisements is as important as the content and design of those advertisements. A fast and efficient response to both requests for information and applications will do much to promote a positive image for the school, while a bureaucratic system will have the opposite effect.

Many schools slow things down by asking applicants to send a stamped addressed envelope if they want details of the post. This penny-pinching procedure reduces the amount of time available before the specified closing date. It is far better to include a fax or 24-hour answerphone number in the job advertisement, as long as these actually work!

Shortlisting

The job description and the person specification should be used to set the criteria and standards for deciding which candidates to shortlist for interview. The information that candidates have provided in their application forms can then be judged against these criteria. Using a simple scoring system and entering candidates' scores on a grid will speed up this process and ensure that it is carried out consistently.

Shortlisting grid

Job title:	Head of science					
Main responsibilities	Name	Name	Name	Name	Name	Name
1. Teaching						
2. Monitoring pupil attainment						
3. Managing staff						
4. Curriculum development						
5. Finance and resource management						
Total						

Scoring system:

0 **No evidence** of relevant experience/qualifications/ qualities

1 **Minimal evidence**

2 **Some evidence**, but only of limited responsibility or in a different type of school

3 **Fair amount of evidence**

4 **Strong evidence**

5 **Very strong evidence** - probably already in a similar post

Taking up references

Some schools ask for references for all shortlisted candidates. However, since references contain judgements that are essentially subjective, there is a strong case for using them only to confirm decisions that have already been made. If references are requested for all shortlisted candidates, it is probably best to impose a structure on them by asking questions directly related to the selection criteria.

Interpreting a reference, especially one that has not been structured by the recruiting school, can present difficulties. Some headteachers let candidates see their own references, and in our opinion they are quite right to do so. However, since these 'open' references are sometimes less frank than traditional 'closed' references, it is important that schools know which kind they are dealing with.

An additional problem with references concerns the unwritten rules that have grown up around them - in the education service at least. Over the years, phrases such as "strongly recommended as a candidate worthy of serious consideration" have come to be a coded way of warning recruiters off particular candidates. The phrase "recommended without reservation", on the other hand, is usually meant as a genuine recommendation. The trouble is that school governors and headteachers may not always be familiar with this code, and its use can lead to misunderstandings. Therefore, references should be treated with caution.

CHAPTER 4
INTERVIEWS AND THEIR ALTERNATIVES

Uses and abuses of the interview process

The job interview, while being the most widely used selection tool, is also the most open to abuse. All too often, candidates will come out of an interview feeling that their time has been wasted, that their ability to do the job has not actually been assessed and that interviewers did not seem to know what they were looking for.

Many organisations, including some schools, subject job candidates to irrelevant and discriminatory questions about their personal lives. Lack of training in interview techniques and equal opportunities issues also means that interviewers often base their decisions on subjective criteria such as appearance, dress and whether they 'hit it off' with candidates. As long ago as 1964, a research study found that it takes interviewers, on average, just under four minutes to make a decision, while they spend the rest of the interview looking for information to confirm that first impression (Webster EC, 1964, *Decision making in the employment interview*, Montreal: Industrial Relations Centre, McGill University). More recently, some studies have concluded that selection interviews are no better at predicting a candidate's ability to do a particular job than graphology or even astronomy. However, such findings may say more about the way job interviews are often conducted than about their intrinsic validity as a selection method.

Panel interviews are intended to ensure that decisions are based on a variety of perspectives, rather than the prejudices of one individual, but they have their own difficulties. In particular, a panel that is too large can intimidate candidates and become unwieldy. We therefore suggest that an interview panel should consist of no more than three or at most four interviewers, unless particular circumstances warrant a larger number.

We give detailed guidance on how to prepare for and conduct effective interviews later in this chapter, but first you should consider whether alternative approaches may be appropriate for the post that is vacant.

Alternative selection methods

Despite its potential problems, the formal panel interview is likely to remain the most widely used method of selecting staff in schools. When carefully planned and structured and carried out by trained and competent interviewers, it is an efficient and cost-effective way of collecting certain types of information, for example about candidates' qualifications and past work experience. However, as it is not the most reliable way of gathering information about other important characteristics, including aptitude, it is often advisable to supplement the interview with other selection methods.

Work sampling

It is now very common for schools to ask candidates for teaching posts to give demonstration lessons. Work sampling, as this technique is known, can be a more effective way of discovering if someone has the skills to do a particular job than any number of interview questions, but like any other selection method it has to be carefully planned. Putting a succession of candidates in front of the same Year 9 class on a hot summer's day is clearly unfair both to the pupils and the candidates themselves - especially those expected to teach at the end of the afternoon. A preferable approach is to ask candidates to teach different classes from the same year group.

Letters inviting candidates to interview should indicate the age and ability levels of the pupils they will be teaching and the arrangements for observing their work. In some schools, single observers will work on a rota system, each observing part of a lesson. In other schools, observers will work in a team. Whatever system is used, it is important that all observers know exactly what they are looking for, whether that be an ability to motivate pupils, a particular style of teaching or specialist subject knowledge.

It is also important that those who evaluate teaching demonstrations have had thorough training in classroom observation techniques. Lay governors have a key role to play in assessing candidates' 'life skills', but classroom observation is best left to the professionals.

It will often be clear at the end of a sample lesson that a candidate is not suited for a particular job. Some schools, therefore, reduce the shortlist at the end of this part of the process, and interview only those candidates who have already demonstrated a strong aptitude for the job.

Work sampling is not yet widely used in the selection of non-teaching staff in schools. However, there is no reason why candidates applying for a job as a school secretary, for example, should not be set practical tasks such as word processing letters and dealing with telephone callers. Similarly, candidates for a caretaker's job might be set tasks designed to establish how well they can prioritise work.

Psychometric tests

Psychometric tests have grown in popularity in recent years. These standardised methods of assessing candidates are often viewed as fairer and less potentially discriminatory than selection interviews. Certainly, if tests are properly designed and administered, they can provide a useful supplement to more traditional selection methods.

The tests fall into two main categories. Aptitude tests are used mostly to predict future performance in very specific areas. Examples would include tests to assess numeracy and the ability to use computers for specific tasks. The use of these tests for assessing candidates for teaching posts is limited, though they may be relevant for some clerical posts in schools.

The second type of test is designed to provide information about personality and motivational characteristics. These personality tests can help to assess how well a candidate might work with other members of a team, and are particularly useful if the whole team has been tested. The costs of administering personality tests means that schools are most likely to use them when selecting headteachers and other senior members of staff.

The use of many tests is protected by the British Psychological Society's standards, which require testers to be registered and trained. However, with dozens of psychometric tests on the market, schools need to make their choice with care, preferably with the help of their personnel adviser.

Simulations

In-tray exercises, presentations and other practical exercises can help selectors to discover how a candidate might carry out specific tasks. Rather than buying these exercises 'off the shelf', schools should devise their own, making sure that they are directly related to the job. Selectors also need to think through what they are looking for and what constitutes a good or bad answer.

Group exercises

Group problem-solving exercises or discussions can be used for assessing candidates' interpersonal skills and ability to argue logically. These exercises are especially relevant for senior appointments, but again care must be taken that they are relevant to the job.

Information from candidates' existing schools

Visits to candidates' current schools are worth considering, especially for senior appointments, though this is obviously a costly and time-consuming method of gathering information. An alternative is to look at inspection reports, 'league tables' and other publicly available information about candidates' existing schools. Of course, not all schools have had recent inspections, but provided this type of information is viewed with caution and candidates are treated equally, it can provide valuable insights into their experience and achievements.

Presentations of candidates' work

Another method of finding out about candidates' performance in their current role is to ask for examples of reports, teaching materials or projects that they have produced. Candidates can either be asked to send these materials with their applications or to discuss them on the day of the interview. As well as providing some concrete evidence of past achievements, this is a good way of making candidates feel that they have been given the chance to prove what they can do.

Pupil feedback

A few schools now involve pupils in staff appointments, with some going so far as to give pupil representatives the chance to interview shortlisted candidates. Other schools invite pupil feedback on candidates' practical teaching demonstrations. The success of these methods will obviously depend on pupils' good sense and maturity, but those schools that have allowed pupils to play a part in staff selection have generally been pleasantly surprised by the way that they have risen to the challenge.

The 'peas on knife' or 'death by sherry' test

A social event where people with an interest in the appointment are invited to meet the candidates is sometimes part of the selection process. This is a way of widening the number of people involved in staff selection, but it can be difficult to give all of the candidates the same opportunity to speak to everyone. Unless managed very skilfully, the social event can also seem stilted and false.

Deciding which methods to use

The above selection methods can help schools to identify qualities and abilities that may not emerge at interview. However, selectors need to weigh up the relative worth of each method and consider its contribution to the overall selection process before deciding whether to adopt it.

Checklist for evaluating alternative selection methods

- What does this method add to the interviewing process?
- How will it help to meet the objective of selecting the best candidate?
- What are the difficulties associated with this method?
- Can it be organised in a way that is fair to all candidates?
- Can candidates' performance be rated fairly and consistently?

Preparing to interview

Whether or not any supplementary methods are used, the formal panel interview will probably be the centrepiece of the selection process. As with any complex activity, preparation is essential.

Interview skills training needs to take place long before a vacancy has even arisen, with appropriate courses for governors and other interviewers. The aim of the training should be to help interviewers to assess candidates as objectively as possible and guard against the possibility of their personal preferences and prejudices affecting the outcome of the interview. Courses need to cover questioning and assessment techniques, as well as implementing those aspects of equal opportunities and employment law that we looked at in Chapter 2 of this book.

Practical arrangements

If interviews are to proceed smoothly, it is important to pay careful attention to the following:
- Have you given candidates clear instructions about the time and place of the interview?
- Have you told candidates what information and examples of work they will need to bring with them, whether they will be expected to take any tests and whether a decision will be made on the day?

- Have you informed candidates of the form the interview will take and how long it will last?
- Have you made sure that candidates will be properly welcomed when they arrive, given a comfortable place to wait and offered refreshments?
- Have you provided appropriate facilities for candidates with disabilities?

Planning the interview

Once the practical details have been worked out, preparations for the interview itself can begin. These preparations need to be informed by the aims of the interview, which are:

- to determine the suitability of each candidate for the job;
- to provide candidates with accurate information about the job and the school;
- to ensure that both successful and unsuccessful candidates leave with a positive impression of the school.

A carefully planned and structured interview will help to ensure that all important information is covered and that candidates are treated fairly and consistently. The same selection criteria that have already been used to shortlist candidates should now be used to determine the structure of the interview. During the planning stage, interviewers also need to consider their own roles and responsibilities so that no one interviewer ends up dominating the proceedings.

Suggested structure for a panel interview

Chair:
- welcomes the candidate and introduces the other panel members;
- outlines the interview structure and sets the scene, for example by summarising the key elements of the job and explaining why the vacancy has arisen;
- gets the candidate talking by asking a few fairly general, open-ended questions.

Interviewer 2:
- asks about the candidate's past work experience and training.

Interviewer 3:
- establishes what experience the candidate has of the duties listed in the job description and tries to discover how well the candidate would perform each one.

Chair:
- seeks clarification on any issues not fully covered by previous answers;
- provides information on pay, conditions of service and similar matters;
- invites questions from the candidate;
- asks if the candidate wishes to add any information;
- explains when a decision will be made;
- closes the interview and thanks the candidate for attending.

Preparing interview questions

To ensure that candidates are asked only for relevant information, questions should relate directly to the selection criteria detailed in the job description and person specification. These two crucial documents will also help interviewers to follow the same line of questioning with each candidate and avoid questions about candidates' personal lives, which are almost always inappropriate.

However, while interviewers need to aim for a consistent approach, it is not usually practical to ask each candidate exactly the same questions. Some standard questions can be prepared in advance, but interviewers need to respond to what individual candidates have said, for example by asking them to clarify or expand on particular points.

Conducting the interview

The interview should give candidates the opportunity to provide as much information as possible about their ability to do the job. Therefore, interviewers need to establish a rapport with each candidate early on in the interview by adopting a friendly manner but not by being overly-friendly or patronising. They should show interest in what the candidate is saying and avoid discouraging actions such as looking at the clock or shuffling papers. They also need to let the candidate do most of the talking and listen attentively.

At the same time, interviewers need to be sensitive to cross-cultural issues and not allow cultural assumptions to cloud their judgements. For example, a candidate who greets interviewers with a firm handshake and looks them straight in the eye is not necessarily going to make a better teacher than one who comes from a background where such behaviour is deemed the height of bad manners.

Some 'Dos' and 'Don'ts' for interviewers

DO try to put candidates at their ease.

DO ask questions that test candidates' suitability in terms of the qualifications, skills, aptitude and experience identified as necessary for the job.

DO listen and make sure that the candidates do most of the talking.

DO ask open questions; for example "What are the key responsibilities in your current role?"

DO NOT ask too many closed questions that will elicit only a "Yes" or "No" answer.

DO NOT ask leading questions such as: "You're obviously committed to the concept of child-centred learning, aren't you?"

DO NOT ask questions about candidates' domestic situation unless these are directly related to the job, which they are likely to be only in residential situations. (To ask a woman candidate about her child-care arrangements or partner's job, without putting the same questions to male candidates may be discriminatory.)

DO NOT ask questions relating to candidates' ethnic origin.

DO NOT ask disabled candidates unnecessary questions about the nature of their disability.

DO NOT express your own opinion or argue with candidates and/or other interviewers.

Taking interview notes

It is important to record the evidence that comes out in an interview. Notes should relate to the pre-determined selection criteria, rather than to interviewers' subjective impressions.

Appointment of head of subject in a secondary school - interviewers' notes

Interviewer	Candidate A	Candidate B	Candidate C
Question 1: What experience do you have of assessment at KS3 and its links to KS2?			
1	"All staff work together, assessment in class." Woolly answer	"Aware of primary school links (KS 1,2,3). Happy this is done within context of the classroom. Assess older children."	Experience in primary liaison across the board, in-depth understanding of assessment. Good answer
2	"Use form to assess in class context. Regular monitoring KS3 results." Needed prompting	"Primary liaison - own assessment. Collect info." Good answer	Aware of primary school needs and links only. Brief answer
3	"Forms. Assessment in class." Not convincing	"Primary visits - make own assessments as well as using primary school data." Good understanding and process, v. lengthy answer	"Knowledge of primary assessment, monitoring within class." Reasonable answer
Question 2: How would you judge whether the quality of teaching in your department is satisfactory?			
1	Not much idea. "Occasional observation." Not a manager	"Watching teachers teach, give positive feedback." Lack of depth	"Peer observation more important than a managerial framework."
2	"Would observe when time permits." Very unconvincing	"Watch teachers, the importance of feedback." Very brief	"Managers can be threatening, peer observation between teachers."

Looking at these interviewers' notes, it is difficult to see why Candidate B was appointed. Had the interviewers made a list of key words or phrases that they would expect to hear, they could have ticked these off, and their notes might then have shown more clearly why Candidate B was selected in preference to the two others.

It would also have been clearer if the written record of the interview had shown that a scoring system had been used.

How to take notes at an interview

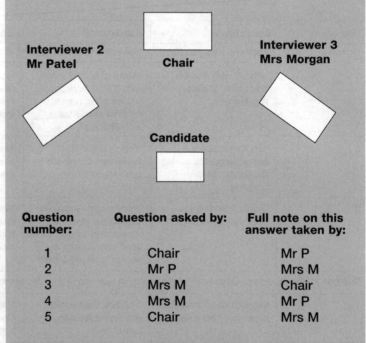

It is better not to attempt to take full notes on all of the questions asked because you will not be able to maintain concentration at a high enough level for that length of time. Do not try to write notes and ask questions at the same time. Instead, when planning the questions that each interviewer will ask, decide who will minute the answer to each question, as below.

Interviewer 2
Mr Patel

Chair

Interviewer 3
Mrs Morgan

Candidate

Question number:	Question asked by:	Full note on this answer taken by:
1	Chair	Mr P
2	Mr P	Mrs M
3	Mrs M	Chair
4	Mrs M	Mr P
5	Chair	Mrs M

This ensures, for example, that Mr Patel has a comprehensive note on the answers to Question 1 for all candidates.

Assessing the candidates' performance

The selection criteria used to structure the interview and formulate questions should now be used to assess the candidates. A standard assessment form, similar to the one suggested for the shortlisting process (see Chapter 3) can be used to record how closely each candidate matches the selection criteria.

In the interests of fairness and consistency, this assessment should take place only after all the interviews have been completed, with the whole interviewing panel discussing each candidate in turn. This is an important point, as employment tribunals hearing claims for unlawful discrimination may take a critical view of individual panel members coming to their own decisions before the panel as a whole has discussed the candidates.

Assessment should be based on information gathered at all stages of the selection process, including:
- candidates' application forms;
- any tests they have taken;
- any other selection methods that have been used;
- the interview itself;
- references (these should be used primarily to confirm information from other sources).

An unfortunate choice

After three years' successful experience of teaching in a suburban primary school with well-motivated pupils and an active parent teacher association, Liz Smith was appointed to a much larger school in an inner-city area. The school had gone through a standard recruitment and selection procedure but both the job description and person specification had been couched in very general terms.

Within a few weeks of Mrs Smith's appointment, it became clear that she was not finding her feet as quickly as the headteacher and governors had expected. She appeared to have difficulty establishing appropriate relationships with pupils, some of whom were becoming disruptive. Worried parents began to complain.

The school could have avoided these problems by identifying the particular needs of its pupils more closely and spelling out how the successful applicant would be expected to meet those needs. Skilled questioning might then have shown whether Mrs Smith had the ability to take on the challenge that some of the school's pupils presented. However, there is often a gap between what people say they can do and what they actually can do. So, simply asking Mrs Smith how she would deal with particular situations would not have given interviewers all the information they needed. A teaching demonstration in front of some of the school's pupils would been more helpful, as long as it was evaluated by someone with the necessary skills and experience.

As it happens, in this case, Mrs Smith and the other candidates had been asked to give short teaching demonstrations, but these had been observed by a governor who had no teaching experience or training in classroom observation. This error of judgement by the school's managers meant that the unfortunate outcome of the appointment was fairly predictable.

Debriefing candidates after the interview process

It is good practice to offer unsuccessful candidates a debriefing session at the end of the interview day. This should be carried out by an experienced member of the interviewing panel, often the headteacher, who may find the following plan useful.

Plan for debriefing candidates

Identify the candidate's strengths and successes.

Advise on areas where more experience is needed, whether qualifications need strengthening, and if awareness of any issues needs raising.

Review any interview answers or comments that were inappropriate or not well received, and specify parts of the interview where presentation and/or performance was inadequate.

Invite feedback on the school's selection process.

Thank the candidate for their application and wish them well for the future.

CHAPTER 5
APPOINTING HEADTEACHERS AND DEPUTIES

The appointment of a headteacher is probably the most important task a governing body ever has to carry out. As the leading professional in any school, the headteacher is responsible not only for its day-to-day management but also for providing the leadership and vision needed to make sure that pupils receive the best possible education. The appointment of a headteacher is therefore too important to be left to chance or subjective judgements, but needs to be approached with even greater care and rigour than other appointments. The same goes for the recruitment and selection of deputy heads, who in all but the smaller schools are responsible for developing key policies and practices and managing the resources used to achieve the school's aims and objectives. Poor selection decisions at these very senior levels will almost certainly have disastrous results for the school and its pupils.

The crucial role of headteachers and deputies is recognised by education law, which lays down detailed requirements for their appointment. These requirements do not cover the appointment of assistant headteachers, but we would advise schools to apply a similar degree of rigour when considering candidates for these recently created positions, and indeed all senior management jobs.

The legal framework

Section 16 of the Schools Standards and Framework Act 1998 lays down the following requirements for the appointment of headteachers and deputy heads in community, voluntary controlled and community special schools:

- The school's governing body must notify the LEA of any vacancy for a headteacher or deputy headteacher.
- The local authority's director of education or his or her representative is entitled to attend all proceedings relating to these appointments and has a duty to give advice. All of those involved in the selection process are obliged to consider that advice, but not necessarily to follow it.
- The governing body must appoint a selection panel of at least three governors. This selection panel then controls its own proceedings but decisions must be made by a majority of its members. (Since no member of the panel can have a casting vote in the event of a tie, we would recommend that the panel should consist of an uneven number of governors.)
- The governors must advertise the vacancy in an appropriate national publication.
- The selection panel should shortlist applicants as it thinks fit.
- If appropriate, the selection panel recommends one of the interviewed applicants to a meeting of the full governing body, which must be quorate.
- If the governing body approves, the successful applicant is recommended to the LEA. The LEA must appoint this individual unless he or she does not meet statutory requirements relating to qualifications, health and physical capacity, or fitness on educational or other grounds.
- If the selection panel cannot agree or the governing body does not approve its recommendation, the governors should re-advertise the post.
- If it appears that the post will not be filled in the short-term, the governors may recommend a person for appointment as acting headteacher or acting deputy headteacher. Alternatively, the governors may engage a person to provide services other than under a contract of employment with the LEA, for example under a consultancy arrangement.

Section 17 of the School Standards and Framework Act covers the appointment of headteachers and deputies in foundation, voluntary aided and foundation special schools. Where such schools have given advisory rights to their LEA, the procedures that need to be followed are very similar to those outlined above. The key difference is that the selection panel makes its final recommendation not to the LEA, but to the full governing body, which is the employer in law as well as in practice in these schools.

Where a foundation, voluntary aided or foundation special school has not given the LEA advisory rights in respect of the appointment of headteachers and deputy heads, the selection panel must still notify the LEA of the names of shortlisted applicants. However, since in this situation the director of education is not entitled to attend the appointment interviews, the selection panel's notification must include enough information about each of the shortlisted candidates to enable the LEA to determine his or her suitability for the appointment.

The selection process

The importance of headteacher and deputy head appointments and the legal requirements surrounding them means that they are likely to be considerably more complex and time-consuming than the appointment of other staff. The following schedule outlines the key stages in this process and the time each one is likely to take.

Schedule for appointing a headteacher or deputy

1. Full governing body meeting
The governing body holds a mandatory meeting to agree the appointment process and nominate a selection panel.
Time: 2-3 hours

2. Training/briefing for selection panel
The appointment of a headteacher is a rare event in most schools, and few governors are likely to have much experience of the process. Therefore, we suggest that the school's personnel adviser or another suitably

qualified person is asked to provide a training session covering interviewing techniques and processes.
Time: 2-3 hours

3. Preparing information for applicants
The selection panel is responsible for preparing an advertisement and an applicant's information pack containing:
- information about the school;
- the job description;
- the person specification;
- an application form.

Time: considerable. Best to allow several weeks for the completion of these tasks.

4. Advertising
The advertisement is placed in a national newspaper, usually five days before its appearance (but longer if artwork is to be included) with a closing date at least 14 days later.
Time: Minimum 19-day turnround

5. Shortlisting
The selection panel meets after the closing date to draw up a shortlist and call references for selected candidates. When appointing a deputy headteacher, the governors will usually wish to take advice from the headteacher on the shortlisting procedure.
Time: 4 hours

6. Re-advertising
If there are insufficient suitable candidates, the selection panel will need to re-advertise the job.
Time: Minimum 19-day turnround, as before

7. Invitation to interview
Chair of selection panel writes to shortlisted candidates, inviting them to interview and giving details of interview schedule.
Time: 5-day turnround

8. Interviews: Day 1
- Tour of school and briefing. Time: 1-2 hours
- First round of interviews, possibly conducted by

two to four different interview panels made up of staff, governors and LEA representatives. Time: 3-4 hours
● Psychometric testing and/or in-tray exercise and/or presentation. Time: 1 hour each
● Possible social event bringing together candidates, staff, governors, PTA etc. Time: 1-2 hours

9. Selection for final interview
Selection panel meets to decide on which candidates should go forward to the second round of interviews. Time: 1-2 hours

10. Interviews: Day 2
Final interviews conducted by the selection panel, with LEA advisers present where appropriate.
Time: 1 hour per interview

11. Offer of appointment
Chair of selection panel makes an offer of appointment to the selected candidate, subject to staff qualification requirements, medical and criminal records check and ratification by full governing body. Other candidates debriefed.
Time: 20 minutes per candidate

12. Full governing body agrees the appointment
The governing body meets to ratify the selection panel's decision.
Time: 1 hour

Job descriptions

A job description for a headship is likely to be based on the eight generic functions carried out by any headteacher. These are:
● teaching;
● management of pupil's attainment and progress;
● management of the curriculum;
● management of staff;
● financial management;
● management of resources and premises;
● management of the school within the community;
● management and governance.

Individual job descriptions will obviously place more emphasis on some of these functions than on others. For example, teaching is likely to form a greater part of the headteacher's job in a small primary school than in a large secondary school, while the management of resources and premises may be particularly important for a school that is embarking on major building works.

The model job description below can be modified to take account of an individual school's circumstances. It can also be adapted for the appointment of a deputy head, who would be expected to assist the head in carrying out some or all of the eight generic functions. A deputy's exact role will, of course, depend on the size of the school and the type of management it has. In a school with two or three deputy heads, each will be expected to specialise in specific areas. Where there is only one deputy, he or she will usually have a broader role.

Model job description for a headteacher appointment

The headteacher will carry out his or her professional duties in accordance with the national Conditions of Employment for headteachers and all relevant employment and education legislation.

The headteacher will be responsible to the governors for the conduct, management and administration of the school, subject to any policies that the Department for Education and Employment or the governors may make. This job description is subject to annual review.

Accountabilities

Teaching
i) Participate, to such an extent as may be appropriate having regard to other duties, in the teaching of pupils at the school, including the provision of cover for absent teachers.

Management of pupils' attainment and progress
i) Determine, implement and monitor systems for tracking and improving pupils' attainment and progress.
ii) Determine and implement standards of behaviour and discipline.

Management of the curriculum
i) Determine, implement and review the curriculum to ensure breadth, balance and relevance to all pupils whatever their abilities, aptitudes and needs.

Management of staff
i) Ensure high standards of teaching.
ii) Lead, motivate, deploy and manage staff.
iii) Establish an appropriate staffing structure and define staff tasks, responsibilities and job descriptions.
iv) Participate in and advise governors on the selection and appointment of high quality staff.
v) Develop and implement policies and procedures for staff development, performance management, appraisal and support.

Financial management
i) Take overall responsibility for the management of the school's financial resources.
ii) Determine short, medium and long-term priorities for the school, having regard to any financial implications and the ability to meet these from foreseen income.

Management of resources and premises
i) Ensure the development, maintenance, security and safety of the pupils, staff, school buildings, grounds and equipment.

Management of the school within the community
i) Establish and maintain links with employers, relevant external agencies and the media.
ii) Represent the school in the local community.
iii) Support and encourage parents' involvement in the life and work of the school through the medium of the Parent Teacher Association and by other appropriate means.
iv) Promote links with feeder primary schools/local secondary schools and their headteachers.

Management and governance
i) Advise and assist the governing body in the exercise of its functions.
ii) Draft the school development plan for consideration by the governing body.
iii) In conjunction with the governing body, develop and implement monitoring and evaluation systems for all aspects of the school.

The person specification

This will also need to relate to the key functions of the headteacher or deputy. In addition, it should spell out the more general qualities the successful applicant will need to demonstrate and indicate whether these are essential or just desirable. Again, the following example can be adapted to the needs of individual schools.

__Model person specification for the appointment of a deputy headteacher with responsibility for the curriculum in a large secondary school__

The successful applicant for this post will be expected to demonstrate the following qualities, skills, knowledge and experience.

General qualities and experience:
- evidence of significant experience and a proven record of achievement as a senior manager in secondary education;
- stamina, energy, drive and confidence;
- capacity for development and evidence of having recently pursued professional development activities;
- evidence of the ability to prioritise work and respond to changing circumstances;
- evidence of the ability to gain and maintain the confidence of colleagues and to show consistency of judgement in decision making.

Teaching:
- substantial and successful teaching experience across the 11-18 age group.

Management of the curriculum:
- evidence of a broad knowledge of the National Curriculum and sound experience of curriculum delivery, monitoring and assessment;
- evidence of the ability to analyse complex curriculum issues and develop effective and creative teaching and learning strategies;
- evidence of the skills necessary to communicate curriculum issues clearly and effectively both to colleagues and others, including parents.

> **Other desirable characteristics:**
> ● In view of the school's current plans for a new learning support centre, an interest in self-managed learning and experience of developing appropriate materials would also be desirable.

Shortlisting

As with all appointments, candidates for headteacher and deputy head posts should be shortlisted only on the basis of information that can be verified. The job description and person specification should be used to set the criteria for inclusion on the longlist and for reducing this to a manageable shortlist of candidates invited to interview.

These criteria must be applied consistently. For example, it would not be acceptable to say that candidates have to show that they are able to analyse complex financial data and then to shortlist a candidate who has clearly never looked at a balance sheet, merely because that individual happens to have other strengths.

A simple scoring system will help to keep subjective judgements at bay and ensure that selection criteria are applied consistently, both at the shortlisting and interview stage.

The following example shows how such a scoring system might be used to assess candidates on one of the key functions of a headteacher: the management of staff.

> *Assessment of candidates: Management of staff function*
>
> **Selection criteria:**
> ● skill in managing, delegating and relating to people;
> ● the ability to handle difficult situations effectively and sensitively;
> ● the ability to inspire high levels of performance in staff;
> ● energy and stamina;
> ● a positive, optimistic and approachable leadership style with a commitment to equal opportunities and continuous improvement.

Scoring system:

0 No evidence of staff management experience.

1 Minimal evidence, i.e. less than two years.

2 Some evidence, but only of very limited responsibility and/or in a different kind of school; little evidence of achievement.

3 Fair amount of evidence, probably more than four years at senior management level; reasonable match of school, some evidence of achievement. Experience of some of the following: induction, INSET, appraisal, equal opportunities, health and safety.

4 Strong evidence, probably more than four years at senior management level, good match for this school, strong evidence of achievement. Involvement at strategic level in induction, INSET, appraisal, recruitment, equal opportunities, health and safety.

5 Strong evidence of outstanding communication skills, creativity and a leadership style showing confidence, consistency, soundness of judgement, problem-solving capacity, adaptability and vision in relation to staff management. Familiarity with the ways in which the management of people may be measured and improved. Experience as a headteacher of a school which provides a good 'training ground' for this school.

The scores awarded to each candidate can be entered on to a grid, as in the following example.

Model longlisting and shortlisting grid with point scoring system

	Name	Name	Name	Name	Name	Name
General qualities						
Teaching						
Pupils' attainment and progress						
Curriculum management						

	Name	Name	Name	Name	Name	Name
Staff management						
Financial management						
Resources and premises						
Community						
Management and governance						
Total						

Interviewing

There are different ways of carrying out job interviews and we suggest that for the purpose of selecting a headteacher or a deputy, a combination of the following should be used:

● **Presentation interviews,** in which candidates make short presentations on pre-determined subjects to small panels of governors and/or senior staff.

● **Group discussions in small pre-arranged groups** can often be carried out in an informal setting and are worth considering as a way of letting as many governors, senior staff and parents as possible meet the candidates. Though less formal than other kinds of interviews, these discussions are still part of the selection process and the same criteria should apply.

● **Formal panel interviews** conducted by the selection panel should come at the end of the selection process.

Other selection methods, including in-tray exercises, psychometric tests and simulations can be used to supplement interviews and provide valuable additional information about the candidates' ability to do the job (see Chapter 4).

Interview questions

The selection panel will find it helpful to prepare a series of questions relating to each key function of the job. Before using these questions, interviewers should decide what they are looking for and how they will discriminate between good and poor answers. Examples of questions are given below, but these should not be followed slavishly as the information candidates provide in the course of the interview may prompt supplementary questions.

Teaching

● Do you think it important that the headteacher teaches?
● How would you judge whether the quality of teaching in the school is satisfactory?
● How would you set about improving/reviewing/changing....... (any area mentioned below):
  ● the level of pupils' engagement, satisfaction and enjoyment?
  ● teachers' expectations of pupils?
  ● effective lesson planning and delivery by teachers?

Management of pupils' attainment and progress

● How would you judge if pupils are achieving as much as they can and progressing as quickly as they can?
● What do you view as the key factors in managing pupils' behaviour?
● How important is homework in reinforcing and extending learning?
● How would you set about changing/improving/reviewing......(any of the areas mentioned below):
  ● pupils' interest and enthusiasm in their work and their standards of behaviour?
  ● pupils' attainment in relation to national standards?
  ● pupils' ability to show initiative and take responsibility?

Management of the curriculum

● How would you set about improving/monitoring/implementing... (any of the following):
  ● the curriculum in relation to pupils with special educational needs?

- equality of access and opportunity?
- extra-curricular provision?
- curriculum planning in relation to providing continuity and progression of learning?
- the use of assessment to inform curriculum planning?

Management of staff

- What is the most difficult staff management issue that you have dealt with? How did you deal with it?
- How would you manage an under-performing member of staff?
- How would you set about improving/monitoring/implementing... (any of the following):
  - staff morale as measured by visitor comment, pupil response, staff comment, absence rates?
  - appropriate INSET provision for all staff?
  - effective deployment of non-teaching staff?

Financial management

- How important is school-generated income?
- How far should the management of finance be delegated?
- How would you set about improving/monitoring/implementing... (any of the factors mentioned below):
  - the proportion of school development targets achieved in financial terms?
  - the cost of educational provision per subject area per pupil?
  - the level of school-generated income?

Management of resources and premises

- How would you judge whether school resources and premises were well managed?
- How would you set about improving/monitoring......(any of the following):
  - the general appearance of the site?
  - the level of provision of specialist accommodation in relation to curriculum requirements?
  - the level of use of resources and premises?

Management of the school within the community

● How would you set about improving/monitoring/implementing...
  (any of the following):
  ● the school's partnership with parents?
  ● links with local employers?
  ● pupils' contribution to the community, including voluntary
    service?

Management and governance

● How would you set about improving/monitoring/implementing...
  (either of the key factors mentioned below):
  ● the governing body's role as a critical friend of the school?
  ● the governing body's statutory responsibilities, in particular
    for the quality of education the school provides?

Assessing and debriefing the candidates

Once all candidates have been interviewed, they should be assessed
against the criteria used throughout the selection process. This final
assessment needs to take into account information gathered from
all the sources that have been used, including application forms,
test results, references and the interview itself. Unsuccessful
candidates for headteacher or deputy headteacher posts will then
need to be debriefed in the same way as candidates for other posts
(see Chapter 4).

APPENDIX A
USEFUL ADDRESSES

Advisory Conciliation and Arbitration Service
ACAS Head Office
Brandon House
180 Borough High Street
London SE1 1LW
Telephone: 020 7396 5100 (Customer Enquiry Line for London region)
For most enquiries, contact your own regional office (under Dept of
Trade and Industry)

British Psychological Society
St Andrew's House
48 Princess Road East
Leicester LE1 7DR
Telephone: 0116 254 9568
Fax: 0116 247 0787
e-mail: mail@bps.org.uk
website: www.bps.org.uk

Chartered Institute of Personnel and Development
35 Camp Road
London SW19 4UX
Telephone: 020 8971 9000 (ask for enquiries)
website: www.ipd.co.uk (accessible to non-members)

Education Personnel Management Ltd
St John's House
Spitfire Close
Ermine Business Park
Huntingdon
Cambs. PE18 6EP
Telephone: 01480 431993
Fax: 01480 431992
e-mail: epm@educ-personnel.co.uk
website: www.epm.co.uk

National Association of Governors and Managers (NAGM)
Suite 1, 4th Floor
Western House
Smallbrook Queensway
Birmingham B5 4HQ
Telephone/Fax: 0121 643 5787
e-mail: governorhq@hotmail.com
website: www.nagm.org.uk

National Governors Council
Glebe House
Church Street
Crediton
Devon EX17 2AF
Telephone: 01363 774377
Fax: 01363 776007
e-mail: ngc@ngc.org.uk
website: www.ngc.org.uk

THE EDUCATION PERSONNEL MANAGEMENT SERIES

Managing Redundancies is the sixth handbook in the series. Other titles include:

Book 1 **THE WELL TEACHER**
promoting staff health, beating stress and reducing absence
by Maureen Cooper
ISBN: 1-85539-058-2

Stress is not peculiar to staff in education, but is a common cause of absence. Large amounts of limited school budgets are spent each year on sick pay and supply cover. This book gives straightforward practical advice on how to deal strategically with health issues through proactively promoting staff health. It includes suggestions for reducing stress levels in schools. It also outlines how to deal with individual cases of staff absence.

Book 2 **MANAGING CHALLENGING PEOPLE**
dealing with staff conduct
by Maureen Cooper and Bev Curtis
ISBN: 1-85539-057-4

Deals with managing staff whose conduct gives cause for concern. It summarises the employment relationships in schools and those areas of education and employment law relevant to staff discipline. It looks at the difference between conduct and capability, and misconduct and gross misconduct, and describes disciplinary and dismissal procedures relating to teaching and non-teaching staff and headteachers.

Book 3 **MANAGING POOR PERFORMANCE**
handling staff capability issues
by Maureen Cooper and Bev Curtis
ISBN: 1-85539-062-0

Explains clearly why capability is important, and gives advice on how to identify staff with poor performance and how to help them improve. Outlines the legal position and the role of governors, and illustrates the various stages of formal capability procedures and dismissal hearings through model letters and real-life case studies. Provides the help you need to give you confidence in tackling these difficult issues.

Book 4 **MANAGING ALLEGATIONS AGAINST STAFF**
personnel and child protection issues in schools
by Maureen Cooper and Bev Curtis
ISBN: 1-85539-072-8

Gives valuable advice on dealing with the difficult issues arising from accusations made against school employees. Through real-life case studies, a clear outline of the legal background, model procedures and a code of conduct for staff, the book shows what schools can do to protect pupils whilst safeguarding staff from the potentially devastating consequences of false allegations. It also details the stages of action for when the allegations are well founded.

Book 6 **MANAGING REDUNDANCIES**
dealing with reduction and reorganisation of staff
by Maureen Cooper and Bev Curtis
ISBN: 1-85539-082-5

Making staff redundant is one of the hardest things that governors and school managers will ever have to do. Any reduction situation is unsettling and this sensitive issue must be handled fairly and carefully. For schools having to face this difficult process, independent advice is given on keeping staff informed of their options, sources of support including the LEA, employment and other relevant legislation and working to the required timescales.

Other Titles from Network Educational Press

THE SCHOOL EFFECTIVENESS SERIES

Book 1: *Accelerated Learning in the Classroom* by Alistair Smith

Book 2: *Effective Learning Activities* by Chris Dickinson

Book 3: *Effective Heads of Department* by Phil Jones & Nick Sparks

Book 4: *Lessons are for Learning* by Mike Hughes

Book 5: *Effective Learning in Science* by Paul Denley and Keith Bishop

Book 6: *Raising Boys' Achievement* by Jon Pickering

Book 7: *Effective Provision for Able & Talented Children* by Barry Teare

Book 8: *Effective Careers Education & Guidance*
by Andrew Edwards and Anthony Barnes

Book 9: *Best behaviour and Best behaviour FIRST AID* by
Best behaviour FIRST AID (pack of 5 booklets)

Book 10: *The Effective School Governor* by David Marriott

Book 11: *Improving Personal Effectiveness for Managers in Schools* by James Johnson

Book 12: *Making Pupil Data Powerful* by Maggie Pringle and Tony Cobb

Book 13: *Closing the Learning Gap* by Mike Hughes

Book 14: *Getting Started* by Henry Liebling

Book 15: *Leading the Learning School* by Colin Weatherley

Book 16: *Adventures in Learning* by Mike Tilling

Book 17: *Strategies for Closing the Learning Gap* by Mike Hughes with Andy Vass

Book 18: *Classroom Management* by Philip Waterhouse and Chris Dickinson

ACCELERATED LEARNING SERIES

General Editor: **Alistair Smith**

Accelerated Learning in Practice by Alistair Smith

The ALPS Approach: Accelerated Learning in Primary Schools by Alistair Smith and Nicola Call

MapWise by Oliver Caviglioli and Ian Harris

The ALPS Resource Book by Alistair Smith and Nicola Call

VISIONS OF EDUCATION SERIES

The Unfinished Revolution by John Abbott and Terry Ryan

The Child is Father of the Man by John Abbott

The Learning Revolution by Jeanette Vos and Gordon Dryden

Wise-Up by Guy Claxton

THE LITERACY COLLECTION

Helping With Reading by Anne Butterworth and Angela White

Class Talk by Rosemary Sage

OTHER TITLES FROM NEP

Effective Resources for Able and Talented Children by Barry Teare

More Effective Resources for Able and Talented Children by Barry Teare

Imagine That... by Stephen Bowkett

Self-Intelligence by Stephen Bowkett